50 Fruit Dishes for Home

By: Kelly Johnson

Table of Contents

- Mixed Berry Parfait
- Watermelon Feta Salad
- Mango Sticky Rice
- Apple Cinnamon Crumble
- Grilled Pineapple Slices
- Strawberry Spinach Salad
- Banana Pancakes
- Peach Cobbler
- Kiwi Yogurt Bowl
- Cherry Clafoutis
- Blueberry Muffins
- Pineapple Fried Rice
- Baked Apples with Honey
- Fruit Tart with Custard
- Melon Prosciutto Skewers
- Raspberry Chia Pudding
- Coconut Mango Smoothie

- Plum Galette
- Orange Glazed Chicken
- Grapefruit Avocado Salad
- Apple Slaw
- Banana Oat Cookies
- Papaya Lime Boat
- Cranberry Orange Scones
- Mango Avocado Salsa
- Strawberry Shortcake
- Frozen Grape Bites
- Baked Pears with Walnuts
- Lemon Ricotta Pancakes
- Blackberry Basil Lemonade
- Caramelized Banana French Toast
- Watermelon Mint Salad
- Apple Butter
- Tropical Fruit Skewers
- Fig and Goat Cheese Toast
- Cherry Tomato & Peach Bruschetta

- Pineapple Smoothie Bowl
- Fruit Spring Rolls
- Orange Almond Cake
- Roasted Grapes and Brie
- Mango Chicken Lettuce Cups
- Pomegranate Couscous
- Apple and Cheddar Quesadillas
- Strawberry Balsamic Crostini
- Peach Smoothie
- Banana Cream Pie
- Citrus Quinoa Salad
- Blueberry Cheesecake Bars
- Grilled Mango Tacos
- Avocado Peach Toast

Mixed Berry Parfait

Ingredients:

- 1 cup strawberries, sliced
- 1 cup blueberries
- 1 cup raspberries
- 2 cups vanilla Greek yogurt
- 1 cup granola
- 1 tsp honey (optional)

Instructions:

1. In a glass, layer yogurt, berries, and granola.
2. Repeat layers until glass is full.
3. Drizzle honey on top if desired.
4. Serve chilled.

Watermelon Feta Salad

Ingredients:

- 3 cups cubed watermelon
- 1/2 cup crumbled feta cheese
- 1/4 cup fresh mint leaves, torn
- 1 tbsp olive oil
- Juice of 1 lime
- Pinch of sea salt

Instructions:

1. Combine watermelon, feta, and mint in a bowl.
2. Drizzle with olive oil and lime juice.
3. Sprinkle with sea salt and toss gently.
4. Serve cold.

Mango Sticky Rice

Ingredients:

- 1 cup glutinous (sticky) rice
- 1 1/4 cups coconut milk
- 1/4 cup sugar
- 1/2 tsp salt
- 1 ripe mango, sliced

Instructions:

1. Soak rice in water for 4 hours, then steam until tender (20–25 mins).
2. Heat coconut milk with sugar and salt until dissolved (do not boil).
3. Mix most of the coconut milk into rice, let sit 10 minutes.
4. Serve with mango slices and remaining coconut milk drizzled on top.

Apple Cinnamon Crumble

Ingredients:

- 4 apples, peeled and sliced
- 2 tbsp sugar
- 1 tsp cinnamon
- 1 tbsp lemon juice

Crumble Topping:

- 1/2 cup rolled oats
- 1/4 cup brown sugar
- 1/4 cup flour
- 1/4 cup butter, melted

Instructions:

1. Preheat oven to 350°F (175°C).
2. Toss apples with sugar, cinnamon, and lemon juice. Place in baking dish.
3. Mix topping ingredients and sprinkle over apples.
4. Bake for 30–35 minutes or until golden and bubbly.

Grilled Pineapple Slices

Ingredients:

- 1 fresh pineapple, sliced into rings
- 2 tbsp honey or brown sugar
- 1/2 tsp cinnamon
- 1 tbsp melted butter

Instructions:

1. Mix honey/sugar, cinnamon, and butter. Brush onto pineapple.
2. Grill slices 2–3 mins per side until charred and caramelized.
3. Serve warm as dessert or with grilled meats.

Strawberry Spinach Salad

Ingredients:

- 4 cups baby spinach
- 1 cup strawberries, sliced
- 1/4 cup red onion, thinly sliced
- 1/4 cup crumbled goat cheese or feta
- 1/4 cup candied pecans or walnuts

Dressing:

- 2 tbsp balsamic vinegar
- 1 tbsp olive oil
- 1 tsp honey
- Salt and pepper to taste

Instructions:

1. Combine salad ingredients in a large bowl.
2. Whisk together dressing ingredients and drizzle over salad.
3. Toss gently and serve immediately.

Banana Pancakes

Ingredients:

- 2 ripe bananas
- 2 eggs
- 1/4 cup flour (optional, for extra fluffiness)
- 1/2 tsp baking powder
- Butter or oil for cooking

Instructions:

1. Mash bananas and mix with eggs, flour, and baking powder.
2. Heat pan with butter. Drop batter in small rounds.
3. Cook 2 mins per side until golden.
4. Serve with syrup, berries, or more banana slices.

Peach Cobbler

Ingredients:

- 4 ripe peaches, sliced
- 1/4 cup sugar
- 1 tbsp lemon juice
- 1 tsp cinnamon

Topping:

- 1/2 cup flour
- 1/4 cup sugar
- 1/2 tsp baking powder
- 1/4 cup milk
- 1/4 cup butter, melted

Instructions:

1. Preheat oven to 350°F (175°C).
2. Toss peaches with sugar, lemon juice, and cinnamon. Place in baking dish.
3. Stir together topping and pour/spread over peaches.
4. Bake 30–35 minutes until golden and bubbly. Serve warm with ice cream.

Kiwi Yogurt Bowl

Ingredients:

- 1 cup plain or vanilla yogurt
- 2 kiwis, peeled and sliced
- 1/4 cup granola
- 1 tbsp honey
- A few fresh mint leaves (optional)

Instructions:

1. Spoon yogurt into a bowl.
2. Top with kiwi slices and granola.
3. Drizzle honey over and garnish with mint.
4. Serve immediately.

Cherry Clafoutis

Ingredients:

- 2 cups fresh or frozen cherries (pitted)
- 3 eggs
- 1/2 cup sugar
- 1/2 cup flour
- 1 cup milk
- 1 tsp vanilla extract
- Powdered sugar (for dusting)

Instructions:

1. Preheat oven to 350°F (175°C). Butter a baking dish and scatter cherries evenly.
2. Whisk eggs, sugar, flour, milk, and vanilla until smooth.
3. Pour batter over cherries.
4. Bake for 35–40 minutes until puffed and golden.
5. Dust with powdered sugar and serve warm or room temp.

Blueberry Muffins

Ingredients:

- 1 1/2 cups flour
- 3/4 cup sugar
- 1/2 tsp salt
- 2 tsp baking powder
- 1/3 cup vegetable oil
- 1 egg
- 1/3 cup milk
- 1 cup fresh blueberries

Instructions:

1. Preheat oven to 375°F (190°C). Line muffin tin.
2. Mix dry ingredients in one bowl, wet in another.
3. Combine quickly then fold in blueberries.
4. Fill muffin cups 2/3 full.
5. Bake 20-25 minutes until golden.

Pineapple Fried Rice

Ingredients:

- 2 cups cooked jasmine rice (day-old preferred)
- 1 cup diced pineapple
- 2 eggs, beaten
- 1/2 cup diced bell pepper
- 1/2 cup green peas
- 2 garlic cloves, minced
- 2 tbsp soy sauce
- 1 tbsp vegetable oil
- Green onions for garnish

Instructions:

1. Heat oil in a wok or pan, scramble eggs, then remove.
2. Sauté garlic, bell pepper, and peas.
3. Add rice, pineapple, soy sauce, and cooked eggs. Stir-fry until heated through.
4. Garnish with green onions and serve.

Baked Apples with Honey

Ingredients:

- 4 apples, cored
- 4 tbsp honey
- 1 tsp cinnamon
- 1/4 cup chopped nuts (optional)

Instructions:

1. Preheat oven to 350°F (175°C).
2. Place apples in baking dish, fill center with honey, cinnamon, and nuts.
3. Bake 25–30 minutes until tender.
4. Serve warm, optionally with ice cream.

Fruit Tart with Custard

Crust:

- 1 1/4 cups flour
- 1/2 cup butter, cold and diced
- 1/4 cup sugar
- 1 egg yolk
- 1–2 tbsp cold water

Custard:

- 2 cups milk
- 3 egg yolks
- 1/2 cup sugar
- 1/4 cup cornstarch
- 1 tsp vanilla extract

Toppings:

- Mixed fresh fruit (berries, kiwi, peaches, etc.)
- Apricot jam (for glaze)

Instructions:

1. Preheat oven to 375°F (190°C). Make crust by cutting butter into flour and sugar, add egg yolk and water, chill, then roll and blind bake for 15 minutes.

2. Heat milk. Whisk egg yolks, sugar, and cornstarch; temper with hot milk, then cook until thick. Stir in vanilla. Cool.

3. Spread custard in cooled crust. Arrange fruit decoratively.

4. Warm apricot jam and brush over fruit for shine.

Melon Prosciutto Skewers

Ingredients:

- 1 cantaloupe or honeydew melon, cut into cubes or balls
- 8 oz thinly sliced prosciutto
- Fresh basil leaves (optional)
- Toothpicks or small skewers

Instructions:

1. Wrap each melon piece with prosciutto.
2. Skewer with basil leaf if using.
3. Chill and serve as a refreshing appetizer.

Raspberry Chia Pudding

Ingredients:

- 1 cup almond milk (or any milk)
- 3 tbsp chia seeds
- 1/2 cup fresh or frozen raspberries
- 1 tbsp maple syrup or honey
- 1/2 tsp vanilla extract

Instructions:

1. Blend raspberries with milk, sweetener, and vanilla.
2. Stir in chia seeds.
3. Refrigerate at least 4 hours or overnight until pudding thickens.
4. Top with extra berries before serving.

Coconut Mango Smoothie

Ingredients:

- 1 ripe mango, peeled and chopped
- 1 cup coconut milk
- 1/2 cup Greek yogurt or plant-based yogurt
- 1 tbsp honey or agave syrup
- 1/2 cup ice cubes

Instructions:

1. Blend all ingredients until smooth.
2. Pour into a glass and serve immediately.

Plum Galette

Ingredients:

- 1 pre-made pie crust or homemade pastry dough
- 4–5 ripe plums, sliced
- 1/4 cup sugar
- 1 tbsp cornstarch
- 1 tsp cinnamon
- 1 egg, beaten (for egg wash)
- Sugar for sprinkling

Instructions:

1. Preheat oven to 375°F (190°C).
2. Toss plums with sugar, cornstarch, and cinnamon.
3. Roll out dough on baking sheet, leaving a 2-inch border.
4. Spread plum mixture in center, fold edges over fruit.
5. Brush crust with egg wash, sprinkle sugar.
6. Bake 35–40 minutes until golden and bubbling.

Orange Glazed Chicken

Ingredients:

- 4 boneless chicken thighs
- Juice and zest of 2 oranges
- 2 tbsp soy sauce
- 1 tbsp honey
- 1 garlic clove, minced
- 1 tsp ginger, grated
- 1 tbsp olive oil

Instructions:

1. Mix orange juice, zest, soy sauce, honey, garlic, and ginger.
2. Marinate chicken 30 mins.
3. Heat oil in pan, cook chicken until golden and cooked through.
4. Pour marinade into pan, reduce to glaze the chicken.
5. Serve with rice or greens.

Grapefruit Avocado Salad

Ingredients:

- 1 large grapefruit, peeled and segmented
- 1 ripe avocado, sliced
- Mixed greens (arugula, spinach)
- 2 tbsp olive oil
- 1 tbsp honey or agave
- Salt and pepper

Instructions:

1. Arrange greens on a plate, top with grapefruit and avocado.
2. Whisk olive oil, honey, salt, and pepper.
3. Drizzle dressing over salad and serve.

Apple Slaw

Ingredients:

- 2 apples, julienned
- 2 cups shredded cabbage
- 1/4 cup mayonnaise
- 1 tbsp apple cider vinegar
- 1 tsp honey
- Salt and pepper

Instructions:

1. Mix mayonnaise, vinegar, honey, salt, and pepper for dressing.
2. Toss apples and cabbage with dressing.
3. Chill for 20 minutes before serving.

Banana Oat Cookies

Ingredients:

- 2 ripe bananas, mashed
- 1 1/2 cups rolled oats
- 1/4 cup chocolate chips or raisins (optional)
- 1 tsp cinnamon
- 1/2 tsp vanilla extract

Instructions:

1. Preheat oven to 350°F (175°C).
2. Mix all ingredients until combined.
3. Drop spoonfuls onto baking sheet lined with parchment.
4. Bake 12–15 minutes until set and lightly browned.

Papaya Lime Boat

Ingredients:

- 1 ripe papaya, halved and seeded
- Juice of 1 lime
- 1 tbsp honey
- 1/4 cup chopped fresh mint
- Optional: Greek yogurt or coconut cream

Instructions:

1. Drizzle papaya halves with lime juice and honey.
2. Sprinkle with fresh mint.
3. Add a dollop of yogurt or coconut cream if desired.
4. Serve as a refreshing breakfast or snack.

Cranberry Orange Scones

Ingredients:

- 2 cups flour
- 1/4 cup sugar
- 1 tbsp baking powder
- 1/2 tsp salt
- Zest of 1 orange
- 1/2 cup cold butter, cubed
- 1/2 cup dried cranberries
- 2/3 cup heavy cream
- 1 egg

Instructions:

1. Preheat oven to 400°F (200°C).
2. Mix flour, sugar, baking powder, salt, and orange zest.
3. Cut in butter until crumbly.
4. Stir in cranberries.
5. Whisk cream and egg, add to dry mix.
6. Knead lightly, pat into a circle, cut into wedges.
7. Bake 15–18 minutes until golden.

Mango Avocado Salsa

Ingredients:

- 1 ripe mango, diced
- 1 ripe avocado, diced
- 1/4 cup red onion, finely chopped
- 1 jalapeño, seeded and minced (optional)
- Juice of 1 lime
- 1/4 cup fresh cilantro, chopped
- Salt and pepper to taste

Instructions:

1. Gently toss mango, avocado, red onion, and jalapeño in a bowl.
2. Add lime juice, cilantro, salt, and pepper.
3. Mix carefully to avoid mashing the avocado.
4. Serve with tortilla chips or as a topping for grilled fish or chicken.

Strawberry Shortcake

Ingredients:

- 2 cups strawberries, sliced
- 1/4 cup sugar
- 2 cups all-purpose flour
- 1/4 cup sugar (for shortcake)
- 1 tbsp baking powder
- 1/2 tsp salt
- 1/2 cup cold butter, cubed
- 2/3 cup milk
- Whipped cream

Instructions:

1. Toss strawberries with 1/4 cup sugar and let sit 30 mins.
2. Preheat oven to 425°F (220°C).
3. Mix flour, sugar, baking powder, and salt. Cut in butter until crumbly.
4. Stir in milk until just combined.
5. Drop dough by spoonfuls onto baking sheet and bake 12–15 mins until golden.
6. Split shortcakes, fill with strawberries and whipped cream. Serve immediately.

Frozen Grape Bites

Ingredients:

- 2 cups seedless grapes
- Optional: yogurt or melted chocolate for dipping

Instructions:

1. Wash grapes and pat dry.
2. Optional: Dip grapes in yogurt or chocolate and place on parchment paper.
3. Freeze grapes on a baking sheet for at least 2 hours.
4. Serve frozen as a refreshing snack.

Baked Pears with Walnuts

Ingredients:

- 4 pears, halved and cored
- 1/4 cup walnuts, chopped
- 2 tbsp honey
- 1 tsp cinnamon

Instructions:

1. Preheat oven to 350°F (175°C).
2. Place pear halves in a baking dish, sprinkle with walnuts and cinnamon.
3. Drizzle with honey.
4. Bake 25–30 minutes until tender.
5. Serve warm, optionally with yogurt or ice cream.

Lemon Ricotta Pancakes

Ingredients:

- 1 cup ricotta cheese
- 1 cup all-purpose flour
- 1 tbsp sugar
- 1 tsp baking powder
- 1/4 tsp salt
- 3/4 cup milk
- 3 eggs, separated
- Zest and juice of 1 lemon
- Butter or oil for cooking

Instructions:

1. In a bowl, mix ricotta, flour, sugar, baking powder, salt, milk, egg yolks, lemon zest, and juice.
2. Beat egg whites until stiff peaks form, fold gently into batter.
3. Heat butter in a skillet, cook pancakes 2–3 minutes per side until golden.
4. Serve with maple syrup or fresh berries.

Blackberry Basil Lemonade

Ingredients:

- 1 cup fresh blackberries
- 1/4 cup fresh basil leaves
- 1 cup freshly squeezed lemon juice
- 1/2 cup sugar (or to taste)
- 4 cups cold water
- Ice

Instructions:

1. Muddle blackberries and basil together in a pitcher.
2. Add lemon juice, sugar, and water. Stir until sugar dissolves.
3. Strain if desired or leave pulp for texture.
4. Serve over ice and garnish with basil leaves.

Caramelized Banana French Toast

Ingredients:

- 4 slices thick bread (brioche or challah)
- 2 bananas, sliced
- 2 tbsp butter
- 2 tbsp brown sugar
- 2 eggs
- 1/2 cup milk
- 1 tsp vanilla extract
- Cinnamon to taste

Instructions:

1. Whisk eggs, milk, vanilla, and cinnamon.
2. Dip bread slices in egg mixture, cook on skillet until golden.
3. In another pan, melt butter, add bananas and brown sugar. Cook until caramelized.
4. Serve French toast topped with caramelized bananas.

Watermelon Mint Salad

Ingredients:

- 4 cups cubed watermelon
- 1/4 cup fresh mint leaves, chopped
- Juice of 1 lime
- 1 tbsp honey (optional)
- Pinch of salt

Instructions:

1. Combine watermelon and mint in a bowl.
2. Drizzle with lime juice and honey, sprinkle salt.
3. Toss gently and serve chilled.

Apple Butter

Ingredients:

- 4 lbs apples, peeled, cored, and chopped
- 1 cup apple cider or water
- 1 cup brown sugar
- 1 tbsp cinnamon
- 1/2 tsp cloves
- 1/2 tsp nutmeg
- 1 tsp vanilla extract

Instructions:

1. Cook apples and cider in a large pot over medium heat until soft, about 30 minutes.
2. Puree with an immersion blender until smooth.
3. Stir in brown sugar and spices.
4. Simmer uncovered on low heat, stirring occasionally, until thickened (1–2 hours).
5. Stir in vanilla. Cool and store in jars.

Tropical Fruit Skewers

Ingredients:

- Pineapple chunks
- Mango cubes
- Kiwi slices
- Strawberries
- Wooden skewers

Instructions:

1. Thread fruit pieces alternately on skewers.
2. Serve chilled with a side of coconut yogurt for dipping.

Fig and Goat Cheese Toast

Ingredients:

- Baguette slices, toasted
- Fresh figs, sliced
- Goat cheese
- Honey
- Fresh thyme or rosemary (optional)

Instructions:

1. Spread goat cheese on toasted baguette.
2. Top with fig slices.
3. Drizzle honey over and garnish with herbs.

Cherry Tomato & Peach Bruschetta

Ingredients:

- Cherry tomatoes, halved
- Ripe peach, diced
- Fresh basil, chopped
- Balsamic glaze
- Olive oil
- Toasted baguette slices

Instructions:

1. Toss tomatoes, peach, basil, olive oil, salt, and pepper.
2. Spoon mixture onto toasted baguette.
3. Drizzle with balsamic glaze and serve.

Pineapple Smoothie Bowl

Ingredients:

- 1 cup frozen pineapple chunks
- 1 banana
- 1/2 cup coconut milk
- Toppings: granola, shredded coconut, chia seeds

Instructions:

1. Blend pineapple, banana, and coconut milk until smooth.
2. Pour into a bowl and top with granola and seeds.

Fruit Spring Rolls

Ingredients:

- Rice paper wrappers
- Mango strips
- Strawberries, sliced
- Cucumber sticks
- Fresh mint leaves
- Peanut sauce or sweet chili sauce

Instructions:

1. Soak rice paper briefly in warm water until pliable.
2. Layer fruit and mint on wrapper, roll tightly.
3. Serve with dipping sauce.

Orange Almond Cake

Ingredients:

- 2 oranges (whole, unpeeled)
- 6 eggs
- 1 1/2 cups almond meal
- 1 cup sugar
- 1 tsp baking powder

Instructions:

1. Boil oranges whole for 1 hour, cool, then blend whole oranges to a puree.
2. Whisk eggs and sugar until fluffy.
3. Fold in almond meal, baking powder, and orange puree.
4. Pour into greased pan and bake at 350°F (175°C) for 40–45 minutes.
5. Cool before serving.

Roasted Grapes and Brie

Ingredients:

- 2 cups seedless grapes
- 1 tbsp olive oil
- 1 tbsp honey
- 8 oz Brie cheese
- Fresh thyme (optional)
- Crackers or baguette slices

Instructions:

1. Toss grapes with olive oil and honey.
2. Roast at 400°F (200°C) for 15–20 minutes until grapes burst and caramelize.
3. Serve warm grapes over Brie with crackers.

Mango Chicken Lettuce Cups

Ingredients:

- 2 cups cooked chicken, shredded
- 1 ripe mango, diced
- 1/4 cup red bell pepper, diced
- 2 green onions, sliced
- 1 tbsp soy sauce
- 1 tbsp lime juice
- 1 tsp honey
- Butter lettuce leaves

Instructions:

1. In a bowl, combine chicken, mango, bell pepper, green onions, soy sauce, lime juice, and honey.
2. Spoon mixture into lettuce leaves.
3. Serve immediately as handheld cups.

Pomegranate Couscous

Ingredients:

- 1 cup couscous
- 1 1/4 cups boiling water or vegetable broth
- 1/2 cup pomegranate seeds
- 1/4 cup chopped fresh parsley
- 2 tbsp olive oil
- Juice of 1 lemon
- Salt and pepper to taste

Instructions:

1. Pour boiling water/broth over couscous in a bowl, cover, and let sit 5 minutes.
2. Fluff couscous with fork and stir in pomegranate seeds, parsley, olive oil, lemon juice, salt, and pepper.
3. Serve warm or chilled.

Apple and Cheddar Quesadillas

Ingredients:

- 2 flour tortillas
- 1 apple, thinly sliced
- 1 cup shredded cheddar cheese
- 1 tbsp butter

Instructions:

1. Heat butter in skillet over medium heat.
2. Place one tortilla in skillet, sprinkle half the cheese, layer apple slices, then remaining cheese.
3. Top with second tortilla.
4. Cook until golden and cheese melts, flipping once.
5. Cut into wedges and serve.

Strawberry Balsamic Crostini

Ingredients:

- Baguette slices, toasted
- 1 cup strawberries, sliced
- 4 oz cream cheese or goat cheese
- 1 tbsp balsamic glaze
- Fresh basil leaves, chopped

Instructions:

1. Spread cheese on toasted baguette slices.
2. Top with strawberries and drizzle balsamic glaze.
3. Garnish with basil and serve.

Peach Smoothie

Ingredients:

- 2 ripe peaches, pitted and sliced
- 1/2 cup Greek yogurt
- 1/2 cup orange juice
- 1 tbsp honey (optional)
- Ice cubes

Instructions:

1. Blend all ingredients until smooth.
2. Serve immediately chilled.

Banana Cream Pie

Ingredients:

- 1 pre-made pie crust, baked
- 3 ripe bananas, sliced
- 2 cups whole milk
- 3/4 cup sugar
- 1/3 cup cornstarch
- 4 egg yolks
- 2 tbsp butter
- 1 tsp vanilla extract
- Whipped cream for topping

Instructions:

1. In a saucepan, whisk sugar, cornstarch, and egg yolks. Slowly add milk, whisking constantly.
2. Cook over medium heat, stirring, until thickened and bubbly. Remove from heat, stir in butter and vanilla.
3. Layer banana slices in pie crust, pour pudding over.
4. Chill pie for at least 4 hours.
5. Top with whipped cream before serving.

Citrus Quinoa Salad

Ingredients:

- 1 cup cooked quinoa, cooled
- 1 orange, peeled and segmented
- 1 grapefruit, peeled and segmented
- 1/4 cup chopped fresh mint
- 2 tbsp olive oil
- Juice of 1 lemon
- Salt and pepper to taste

Instructions:

1. In a large bowl, combine quinoa, orange, grapefruit, and mint.
2. Whisk olive oil, lemon juice, salt, and pepper, then toss with salad.
3. Serve chilled or at room temperature.

Blueberry Cheesecake Bars

Ingredients:

- For crust:
    - 1 1/2 cups graham cracker crumbs
    - 1/4 cup sugar
    - 1/2 cup melted butter
- For filling:
    - 16 oz cream cheese, softened
    - 2/3 cup sugar
    - 2 eggs
    - 1 tsp vanilla extract
    - 1 cup fresh blueberries

Instructions:

1. Preheat oven to 325°F (165°C).
2. Mix crust ingredients, press into a greased 9x9 inch pan. Bake 10 minutes.
3. Beat cream cheese and sugar until smooth. Add eggs one at a time, then vanilla.
4. Fold in blueberries gently. Pour over crust.
5. Bake 35-40 minutes until set. Cool and refrigerate before cutting.

Grilled Mango Tacos

Ingredients:

- 2 ripe mangoes, peeled and sliced
- 8 small corn tortillas
- 1/2 cup red cabbage, shredded
- 1/4 cup fresh cilantro, chopped
- 1 lime, cut into wedges
- 1/4 cup sour cream or Greek yogurt
- 1 tsp chili powder
- Olive oil

Instructions:

1. Brush mango slices with olive oil and sprinkle chili powder. Grill over medium heat 2-3 minutes per side.
2. Warm tortillas on grill or skillet.
3. Assemble tacos with mango, cabbage, cilantro, and a dollop of sour cream.
4. Serve with lime wedges.

Avocado Peach Toast

Ingredients:

- 2 slices whole grain bread, toasted
- 1 ripe avocado
- 1 ripe peach, thinly sliced
- Salt and pepper
- Optional: drizzle of honey or balsamic glaze

Instructions:

1. Mash avocado, spread evenly over toasted bread.
2. Top with peach slices.
3. Season with salt and pepper.
4. Drizzle honey or balsamic glaze if desired.

www.ingramcontent.com/pod-product-compliance
Lightning Source LLC
LaVergne TN
LVHW081325060526
838201LV00055B/2470